ideals®
FRIENDSHIP

More Than 50 Years of Celebrating Life's Most Treasured Moments

Vol. 56, No. 4

"Friendship multiplies the good of life."
—*Balthasar Gracian*

IDEALS—Vol. 56, No. 4 September MCMXCIX IDEALS (ISSN 0019-137X) is pub-
lished six times a year: January, March, May, July, September, and November by
IDEALS PUBLICATIONS INCORPORATED,
535 Metroplex Drive, Suite 250, Nashville, TN 37211.
Periodical postage paid at Nashville, Tennessee, and additional mailing offices.
Copyright © MCMXCIX by IDEALS PUBLICATIONS INCORPORATED.
POSTMASTER: Send address changes to Ideals, PO Box 305300,
Nashville, TN 37230. All rights reserved.

Title IDEALS registered U.S. Patent Office.
SINGLE ISSUE—U.S. $5.95 USD; Higher in Canada
ONE-YEAR SUBSCRIPTION—U.S. $19.95 USD; Canada $36.00 CDN (incl. GST and shipping); Foreign $25.95 USD
TWO-YEAR SUBSCRIPTION—U.S. $35.95 USD; Canada $66.50 CDN (incl. GST and shipping); Foreign $47.95 USD

Subscribers may call customer service at 1-800-558-4343 to make address changes.
Unsolicited manuscripts will not be returned without a self-addressed, stamped envelope.

ISBN 0-8249-1156-3   GST 131903775

Cover Photo
Floral Bouquet
Photo by Nancy Matthews

Inside Front Cover
Young Girls Playing
in a Garden
Henri Lebasque, artist
Christie's Images/Superstock

Inside Back Cover
Flowers for Little Sister
Victor Gilbert, artist
Christie's Images

THE LAST EVE
OF *Summer*

John Greenleaf Whittier

Summer's last sun nigh unto setting shines
Through yon columnar pines,
And on the deepening shadows of the lawn
Its golden lines are drawn.

Dreaming of long gone summer days like this,
Feeling the wind's soft kiss,
Grateful and glad that failing ear and sight
Have still their old delight,

I sit alone and watch the warm, sweet day
Lapse tenderly away;
And, wistful, with a feeling of forecast,
I ask, 'Is this the last?

'Will nevermore for me the seasons run
Their round, and will the sun

Of ardent summers yet to come forget
For me to rise and set?'

Thou shouldst be here, or I should be with thee,
Wherever thou mayst be,
Lips mute, hands clasped, in silences of speech
Each answering unto each.

For this still hour, this sense of mystery far
Beyond the evening star,
No words outworn suffice on lip or scroll:
The soul would fain with soul.

Wait, while these few swift-passing days fulfill
The wise-disposing Will,
And, in the evening as at morning, trust
The All-Merciful and Just.

The solemn joy that soul-communion feels
Immortal life reveals;
And human love, its prophecy and sign,
Interprets love divine.

Come then, in thought, if that alone may be,
O friend! and bring with thee
Thy calm assurance of transcendent Spheres,
And the Eternal Years!

A white oak spreads its canopy in Acadia National Park in Maine. Photograph by Terry Donnelly.

Arrival of Autumn

Arthur Thatcher

The summer's brightness left the sky today

As autumn grays and shadings

    flecked the blue;

The migrant birds collecting in the glens

Prepare to bid their spring retreats adieu.

Beside the rural highways, goldenrod

Still lifts its bloom for butterfly and bee;

The ripened cornfields, nodding

    in the breeze,

Produce brown billows for a land-like sea.

I find a pleasure in the autumn fields

To equal that which came

    with days of spring;

These are glad hours to muse and meditate

And find some birds continuing to sing.

At the Summer Lake State Wildlife Refuge, cattails frame a reflection of an autumn sky. Photo by Dennis Frates.

Autumn Glimpse

June Masters Bacher

There's a little touch of scarlet
Edging leaves that once were green;
And the goldenrod, once common,
Proudly wears a regal sheen.

Though the yellow rose has faded,
It is freshened by the dew;
And the summer haze has lifted—
Autumn's breeze has swept it blue.

God has crowned the earth with glory,
And His goodness covers all.
Though we hear Him at all seasons,
We can see Him in the fall.

OVERLEAF PHOTOGRAPH: The Black River flows through a forest in Wisconsin's Pattison State Park. Photo by Terry Donnelly.

Autumn Vignettes

Blythe Gwyn Sears

Engraved in memory this autumn day
    Are shaggy barnyard igloos built of hay,
A flash of scarlet on a wild bird's coat,
    A spray of song flung from its tiny throat.
Wrinkled persimmons, ripening, abound
    While chinquapins and chestnuts pelt the ground.
In gardens, marigolds and asters keep
    Sun-bathing quietly before they sleep.
Diminuendo of the insect choir
    Reveals the message it will soon retire.
Jack Frost, on tip-toe, waits with lighted fuse
    To set the woods afire in flaming hues.
His touch ignites a drooping vine or tree
    As summer takes its leave reluctantly.
But birds, in serial flight, have gone to sing
    Where buds uncurl in vernal blossoming,
And aspen leaves afloat on drowsy streams
    Are golden boats that bear the summer's dreams . . .
The happy dreams that memory will keep
    While summer is enwrapped in restful sleep.

*Photographer Gay Bumgarner captured the striking
color in this monkshood and Euonymous alatus.*

A RIDE THROUGH THE COUNTRY

Rides through the country were always a much-anticipated event when I was a boy. The automobile had not yet made its way to the farm, so we traveled by horse and wagon. During autumn, county fairs were one of our most popular destinations. I can still recall my first trip to the fair—eighty years ago.

I remember the course we followed, across our hill pasture and through the gate in the stone wall that divided the pasture from a field of buckwheat that had already been cut. Sheaves of grain stood neatly in rows across the long slope. I recall the beauty of the reddish brown stalks glistening in the brilliance of the autumn sun. From the buckwheat field, we passed through a neighbor's meadow and onto a dirt road that wound down the hills to the site of the fair in the village.

First came a tour of the fair and then a picnic in the shade of a row of stately elms that separated the fairgrounds from the property of a farmer who owned the adjoining land.

The excitement of the fair and the picnic were two special highlights of the day, but nothing was more memorable than the ride to get there, by horse and wagon seven miles from farm to fair. Each year, as the sights and smells of autumn reach my senses, nostalgic memories return of that ride through the country. Although sumac and woodbine still color the road banks and old stone walls, the field of buckwheat is now covered in spruce and pine, and the dirt road is a paved thoroughfare.

The team has long since gone, and the wagon in which we rode stands unused in the barn whose age now nears the two century mark. The pasture is no longer grazed, and the grass and berry bushes have yielded to trees. The deer now inhabit the land, and the hills are no longer tilled. And the boy? He is now a silver-haired man with many golden memories.

The author of two published books, Lansing Christman has been contributing to Ideals *for more than twenty years. Mr. Christman has also been published in several American, foreign, and braille anthologies. He lives in rural South Carolina.*

A red horse-drawn wagon in Beech Mountain, North Carolina, awaits its next journey.
Photo by Spencer Jones/FPG International.

ASPENSONG

Evelynn Merilatt Boal

From pale chartreuse
    to saffron hue,
      with every shade between;
In bright bouquets
    arrayed against
      the lush and verdant green
Of pompous pine
    and formal fir
      and stately spruce grown tall.
Their lower limbs
    spread all around
      like trains worn to a ball.
The hills boast yellow
    garlands now;
      and proud of nature's prize,
They play the scales
    of golden tones
      in perfect exercise.

THE SOUND OF AUTUMN

Roy Z. Kemp

Fruit and nut and yellow leaf—
Each returns to earth's warm lap;
Each one tells that life is brief
With each thud and rustling tap.

Autumn with her russet flowers,
Objects falling to the ground,
Speaks of nature's golden hours.
Autumn is a lovely sound!

Aspen trees form a golden tunnel along this rural rode in Telluride, Colorado. Photo by Dick Dietrich.

Grape-Orange Sauce
Dixie Bonner of Franklin, Tennessee

1	medium juice orange
½	cup water
¼	cup butter
2	tablespoons vinegar
1	tablespoon honey

1½	teaspoons instant chicken bouillon granules
⅛	teaspoon ground ginger
1	tablespoon cornstarch
½	cup red grapes, halved and seeded
2	teaspoons orange extract

Using a vegetable peeler, remove the outer layer of the orange peel. Slice enough peel into julienne strips to measure 1 tablespoon. In a small saucepan, place orange peel. Add enough water to cover. Simmer 15 minutes. Drain well and set aside.

Section the orange over a small bowl to catch juice; add orange sections and set aside. In a small saucepan, combine the ½ cup water, butter, vinegar, honey, bouillon granules, and ginger. Bring to a boil, stirring constantly. In a small bowl, combine cornstarch and 1 tablespoon cold water; stir into vinegar mixture. Continue heating, stirring constantly, until thick and bubbly. Heat 1 to 2 additional minutes. Stir in orange sections and juice, orange peel, grapes, and extract. Heat to boiling. Serve over poultry or pork. Makes approximately 1⅔ cups.

Raisin Puffs
Florence Miller of Hummelstown, Pennsylvania

1	cup water
2½	cups raisins
3½	cups all-purpose flour
1	teaspoon baking soda
⅛	teaspoon salt

1	cup shortening
1½	cups granulated sugar, divided
2	eggs
1	teaspoon vanilla

In a small saucepan, heat water to a boil. Stir in raisins. Reduce heat and simmer 15 minutes, stirring occasionally. Drain and set aside to cool.

Preheat oven to 350° F. In a large bowl, sift together flour, baking soda, and salt. Set aside. In a large bowl, cream shortening with 1 cup of the sugar. Add eggs and vanilla; stir well. Slowly add dry ingredients. Mix well. Stir in raisins. Shape dough into 1-inch balls and roll in remaining granulated sugar. Place on ungreased cookie sheets and bake 12 to 15 minutes or until golden. Makes 5 dozen cookies.

Mini Grape Cups
Margaret Diggs of Jonesboro, Georgia

12 large red grapes
¼ cup pistachio nuts, finely chopped

5 ounces cream cheese, softened

Using a sharp knife, slightly trim both ends of each grape. Slice each grape in half crosswise. Using a small melon baller, scoop out the inside of each grape half, leaving enough to keep grape stable.

Place chopped nuts into a shallow bowl. Dip the rim of each grape cup into nuts. Place a heaping ½ teaspoon of cream cheese into the center of a small square of cheese cloth. Wrap cloth around cheese, shaping cheese into a ball. Unwrap the cheese, leaving it on the cloth. Holding the cheese with the cloth, place the ball into a grape cup, then peel off cloth. Repeat with remaining cups, using a clean piece of cloth each time. Makes 2 dozen appetizers.

Stuffed Grape Leaves
Erin Landry of Brandon, Mississippi

50 grape leaves, canned
⅔ cup long-grain white rice
¼ cup dried yellow split peas
5 cups water, divided
1 teaspoon salt, divided
1 cup chopped scallions
½ cup fresh chopped dill
1 tablespoon fresh tarragon, chopped

3 tablespoons fresh mint, chopped
½ cup chopped parsley
½ pound ground meat (lamb, veal, or beef)
Juice of 3 lemons, divided
¼ teaspoon black pepper
1 teaspoon ground cinnamon
¼ cup olive oil
2 tablespoons granulated sugar

Rinse leaves under running water; drain and set aside. In a small saucepan, combine rice, split peas, and 3 cups water. Boil gently over medium heat 20 minutes, stirring occasionally. Add ½ teaspoon salt. Drain. In a large bowl, combine rice and split peas, scallions, dill, tarragon, mint, parsley, meat, and the juice of 1 lemon. Add ½ teaspoon salt, the pepper, and the cinnamon. Mix thoroughly.

Preheat oven to 350° F. Place two layers of grape leaves on the bottom of a well-oiled 9-by-13-inch baking dish. Place 2 grape leaves on top of each other in the palm of one hand. Top with 1 tablespoon stuffing. Roll up the leaves, folding in the ends to secure the stuffing. Place in prepared dish. Repeat with remaining leaves.

In a small bowl, stir together 2 cups water and ¼ cup oil. Pour over grape leaves. Place ovenproof plates on top of the stuffed grape leaves. Cover baking dish with aluminum foil. Bake 1 hour. In a small bowl, combine sugar with the juice of 2 lemons. Drizzle over grape leaves. Cover and return to oven. Bake an additional 30 minutes or until grape leaves are tender. Serve with plain yogurt. Makes 6 servings.

Ladies to Lunch

Margaret Rorke

If you think that some sort of an ailment
Has just suddenly struck at your spouse;
If her efforts permit no curtailment
When it comes to her grooming the house;
If she passes you by in a hurry
As though something had dealt her a punch,
Let me say there's no reason to worry.
She's but having the ladies to lunch.

If the silver is out of seclusion,
And it's rubbed to a shimmering shine;
If the kitchen is fraught with confusion,
And there's no place to pause or recline;
If you feel you've been turned out of clover
While she cries 'cause the crunchies won't crunch;
These are hurdles you'll have to get over,
For she's having the ladies to lunch.

If routine has been set all asunder,
But the fragrance of food is a treat
Till the wife of your life starts to wonder
If you'll go to a restaurant to eat;
If you haven't determined the matter,
You'll be right if you cherish the hunch
That for dinner you'll find on your platter
What the ladies bequeath you from lunch.

A hostess has prepared a lovely table for her guests in Mixed
Roses *by artist Martha Walter. Image from David David
Gallery, Philadelphia/Superstock.*

When I Was Ten or So

Esther Kem Thomas

When I was ten or so
I owned a woods—a river too,
And overhead, it all was mine,
That vast expanse of blue;
Horizons were unlimited
Where I could see and see—
Oh, I was rich in God's estate,
This all belonged to me!

My world was drifting leisurely,
When I was ten or so;
Why, I'd spend hours, still, alone,
And watch the river go;
I knew its shallows and its deeps,
Its gentle undertow;
The place to wade and where to swim
And how the currents flow.

I was a great explorer, then,
And on my hands and knees
Crawled into thickets, dank and cool,
And had my special trees
Where I would climb and sit aloof
Like some prodigious bird;
I knew the make of every nest
And each bird-call I heard!

To reminisce brings longing thought,
A wish to once again
Go wandering through that estate
I claimed when I was ten,
But threads from which we weave our dreams
Shrink with each passing year—
I wouldn't want my river dwarfed
Or my woods to appear

A fringe of trees along a stream;
It was so big to me—
I'll carry in my heart the way
My childish eyes could see!
And when the times seem strenuous,
In memory I'll go,
Meand'ring through the day I knew
When I was ten or so.

A TIME TO TALK

Robert Frost

When a friend calls to me from the road

And slows his horse to a meaning walk,

I don't stand still and look around

On all the hills I haven't hoed,

And shout from where I am, 'What is it?'

No, not as there is a time to talk.

I thrust my hoe in the mellow ground,

Blade-end up and five feet tall,

And plod: I go up to the stone wall

For a friendly visit.

THROUGH MY WINDOW
Pamela Kennedy

Art by Pat Thompson

LONG-DISTANCE FRIENDS

I was browsing in a gift shop the other day and a small wall hanging caught my eye. On a piece of rough board the artist had painted a colorful garden. Small lavender violets clustered in front of a row of daisies. Behind these, roses and snapdragons bloomed. A line of sunflowers stood guard at the garden's border, and in the distance a sheltering bar-rier of evergreens filled the background. Arched over the top of the plaque were the words "Friend-ship Is Life's Garden."

This idea of friendship as a garden intrigued me. I mentally inventoried my friends, deciding who was a sensitive violet, who a cheerful daisy, which ones were elegant roses, and which were practical and optimistic sunflowers. I must admit I even ventured to identify a few weeds in my musings! Then I recalled the row of trees standing in the background of the artist's scene. I'm not sure if these were meant to be included in friendship's garden, but for me they became a powerful image of a very special kind of friend I treasure—my long-distance friends.

Thirty years of marriage to a military man have offered many wonderful opportunities to make new friends and an equal number of occasions to leave them behind as we moved thousands of miles away to a new assignment. Some of my more stationary acquaintances doubt the possibility of maintaining friendships with people one doesn't see for years. I like to tell them distance isn't really a barrier to friendship, it only adds a new dimension to it.

Like the trees in the artist's picture, my long-distance friends offer a sense of perspective to my life. I can see them in memories that tower above the circumstances of today reminding me of times we shared joy, challenge, sadness, and triumph together. Just like the wind and rain and sun shape the development of a tree, my friends helped to shape me by their influence, example, and encouragement.

I met Nan when she was a patient in a hospital where I was doing volunteer work about twenty-five years ago. I felt so sorry for this beautiful mother of six because she suffered from constant pain and was confined to a wheelchair. With the thought of cheering her up, I visited her often, and we spent several hours sharing our thoughts on life and faith. I'm not sure if my immature attempts to offer solace accomplished much in her life, but her wit and wisdom made a profound difference in mine. She gently demonstrated that true joy and peace are more a matter of internal circumstances than external, that a deep and abiding confidence in God transcends our present doubts, and that family is the context in which we learn about love—both giving and receiving. Her words strengthened me like the nourishing rain strengthens the trunk of a tree, enabling it to grow until it is able to withstand a storm without being broken. I have seen Nan only a handful of times since we were first friends, but each time I feel tested by the winds of a storm, I recall her strength and am encouraged to endure with her grace.

Another friend, Terry, was with me twenty years ago when my second son was born. My husband was overseas, and Terry filled in as my labor and delivery coach. She and I shared an incredible experience and will always be joined by that bond of birth. When her army husband was transferred overseas, I grieved like I was losing a member of my family. Although we corresponded by mail, it was fifteen years before we met again, and when that happened we picked up as if we had only been apart for a few weeks! Our children had grown, our lives and circumstances had changed; but, like the towering evergreens, our roots are intertwined at a deep level, and we will always be together there.

In a small Wisconsin town several years ago, Lynn and I raised toddlers together. We shared all the triumphs and trials of toilet training, tumbles, and temper tantrums. We debated the merits of breast and bottle, whole grain and processed, scheduling and spontaneity. At one time we saw each other several times a day, but now we are fortunate to visit once every few years. Our children are now young men and women, but our mutual experiences as new mothers still bind the two of us together. Like the trees we stand apart, but when the winds of chance and circumstance allow, our branches touch once more and our lives intermingle again like the fragrant boughs.

In the garden of friendship, the colorful blossoms blooming the closest may get the lion's share of our attention, but I have learned to also treasure the trees standing in the background. Just like that row of evergreens in the artist's painting, long-distance friends provide both perspective and beauty: the perspective of the past and the beauty of shared memories adding a depth of experience to our lives that only time and patience can produce.

Pamela Kennedy is a freelance writer of short stories, articles, essays, and children's books. Wife of a retired naval officer and mother of three children, she has made her home on both U.S. coasts and currently resides in Honolulu, Hawaii.

Letter to an Old Friend

Helen Barker

Today, old friend, I'm taking time
To write a line or two
And tell you what it's meant to walk
Friendship's path with you.

It's meant companionship and love
When others turned aside,
Help for overwhelming tasks
That flow with every tide.

It's meant when e'er my feet have strayed,
You did not pass me by,
But clasped my lonely hand in yours
And held hope's candle high.

It's meant that worry, fear, and doubt
Were never borne alone;
For years ago, within your heart,
The seeds of care were sown.

It's meant my home, my dress, my ways,
Need not bow to style.
You've thoughtfully overlooked my flaws
With friendship's loving smile.

And now, old friend, I'll close with this,
Just here at the end,
And let you know my life is rich
From knowing you, my friend.

A mailbox in Ontario, Canada, holds friendly messages.
Photo by Kimberly Burnham/Unicorn Stock Photos.

BITS & PIECES

Go, little letter, apace, apace,
    Fly;
Fly to the light in the valley below —
    Tell my wish to her dewy blue eye.
    —ALFRED, LORD TENNYSON

A woman seldom writes her mind,
but in her postscript.
    —SIR RICHARD STEELE

The only work about writing —
It's a very terrible thing —
Is wrapping your stuff and stamping it
And tying it up with string.
    —MARGARET WIDDEMER

The welcome news is in the letter found;
The carrier's not commission'd to expound:
It speaks itself, and what it does contain,
In all things needful to be known, is plain.
    —JOHN DRYDEN

It is by the benefit of letters that absent friends
are in a manner brought together.
    —L. ANNAEUS SENECA

Blessed be letters — they are the monitors, they are also the comforters, and they are the only true heart-talkers.
—D. G. MITCHELL

Letters from absent friends extinguish fear, Unite division, and draw distance near.
—AARON HILL

A stray volume of real life in the daily packet of the postman. Eternal love, and instant payment.
—DOUGLAS JERROLD

Never burn kindly written letters; it is so pleasant to read them over when the ink is brown, the paper yellow with age, and the hands that traced the friendly words are folded over the heart that prompted them.
—from THE ROYAL GALLERY, *1897*

Correspondences are like small-clothes before the invention of suspenders; it is impossible to keep them up.
—SYDNEY SMITH

Friendship

Author Unknown

Friendship needs no studied phrases,
Polished face, or winning wiles.
Friendship deals no lavish praises;
Friendship dons no surface smiles.

Friendship follows nature's diction,
Shuns the blandishments of art,
Boldly severs truth from fiction,
Speaks the language of the heart.

Friendship favors no condition,
Scorns a narrow-minded creed,
Lovingly fulfills its mission,
Be it word or be it deed.

Friendship cheers the faint and weary,
Makes the timid spirit brave,
Warns the erring, lights the dreary,
Smooths the passage to the grave.

Friendship—pure, unselfish friendship—
All through life's allotted span,
Nurtures, strengthens, widens, lengthens
Man's affinity with man.

A heart-shaped wreath holds a few of nature's treasures.
Photo by Nancy Matthews.

To a Dear Friend

Grace V. Watkins

I heard a woman say, "Oh, there can be
Too much of anything," and thought of rain
And sun-bright wind and mountains and the sea.
"Why, even quietness or laughter can
Become a comradeship too full and wide.
Perhaps she's right," I told myself and sighed.

I thought that later I would query you;
But when we stood upon a twilight slope,
Companioned by a rising star, I knew
Without a phrase or word that love and hope
And trust and faithfulness, and all of such
Infinities, could never be too much.

The value of a comforting arm is depicted in Homer Winslow's
GIRLS STROLLING IN AN ORCHARD. *Image from Christie's Images/Superstock.*

A footbridge crosses a pond littered with leaves in the village of Somesville, Maine. Photo by Jeff Gnass.

Prayer: *Dear Lord, thank You for accepting and loving me even when I make mistakes. Help me to be a builder of friendships as I extend that kind of gracious love to others in Your name.*

Pamela Kennedy

He who covers over an offense promotes love, but whoever repeats the matter separates close friends. Proverbs 17:9 (New International Version)

COVERING OFFENSES

Standing in line next to the tabloid display at the grocery store the other day, I learned more than I ever wanted to about several celebrities. Exposing offenses is a business for some; but thousands of years ago, King Solomon made the observation that covering over another's faults promotes love between friends.

Who among us has never done something embarrassing, committed a faux pas or made a poor decision we've later regretted? It is a gracious friend who will not only overlook our failings, but lovingly protect us from the criticism of others. One of my friends works in a large office where constant deadlines push everyone to produce at a rapid pace. Normally my friend completes her projects on time, but she wrote down the incorrect due date on a particular assignment and didn't realize her mistake until the morning of the day she was expected to make her presentation—two days before she was planning to do it. There was no way she could be ready by the two o'clock P.M. meeting. Panicked, she went to a co-worker with her dilemma, and her co-worker came up with a plan to divide the unfinished tasks and complete them in time. Instead of taking the opportunity to expose the errors of a fellow worker, this gracious woman offered to extend herself to cover the faults of her friend.

In our families, our neighborhoods, and communities, we have ample opportunity to exercise the same kind of friendship and love everyday.

When a child fails to do as well as he might, we have the choice to expose his failure or quietly encourage him to do better the next time. When a spouse is thoughtless or doesn't live up to our expectations in some area, we can ridicule him or speak appreciatively of the things he does do well. When there is a general negativity expressed about a person, do we pile on the criticism adding fuel to the fire, or look for opportunities to defend and uplift the victim of gossip? If we desire to promote love, we need to use such opportunities to bind people together, not tear them apart.

In a world where competition is a driving force, it is often difficult to find people who are sensitive to the needs of others. Oftentimes it seems everyone is out to get ahead or promote his own interests, frequently at the expense of someone else. When we see another's failure, it can be tempting to use it for personal advantage. The warning in Solomon's words reminds us, however, that when we give into the temptation to expose another's faults, we end up destroying friendships. How much better it is to treat others as we would like to be treated and cover over their faults with love. None of us is immune to mistakes, but the understanding of a friend helps us move beyond our failures and encourages us to work toward improvement. Are you a friend who creates division by constantly bringing up the weaknesses of others, or do you seek to build up those around you by offering words of forgiveness and love?

Good Neighbors

Hannah Kahn

Without reward or thought of praise,
They do their work in quiet ways:
Homemade soup, fresh-baked bread,
The pillow smoothed for the head,
Garden flowers brought in when
The veil of grief is heavy. Then
They leave in silence, having done
The little things that hold the sun.

Neighbors

Esther Kem Thomas

Some folks can move away and then they're gone.
And when they are, you scarcely can remember
The sort of way their life was patterned on,
And if they left in August or December,
Or how they looked—how easy they were making it,
Or if their hand was warm and firm on shaking it!
Strange how they took their lives and drifted on—
Once they were here, but when they're gone, they're gone!

But other folks can leave and still remain—
Seems like their ways, once loved, are here forever.
The way they spoke or smiled is clear and plain;
Their fellowship from yours no miles could sever.
They made their place, and once they finished making it
There's no erasing, blurring, nor forsaking it!
Steady and clear the fires of friendship burn,
That heart and hearth shall welcome their return!

A lake house welcomes visitors in North Waterford, Maine. Photo by Dick Dietrich.

House of Dreams

Thomas Curtis Clark

Now let us build, my dear, our house of dreams,
Far from the crowd, far from the city's blare;
Where mighty forests breathe untainted air,
Where smoke can never dim the morning gleams.
This road shall lead to sweet serenity,
All cares and burdens lightly cast away.
Great sycamores will shield by night and day;
The sun and stars alone our lives shall see.
There peace shall be; amid the garden gold
Our hearts shall learn of beauty's loving lore;
In daisy fields we shall again explore
The storied realms of youth, and blithely bold
Shall venture forth beneath a larger sky
And talk of faith and heaven and feel God nigh!

Praise will transform the humblest dwelling into a hallowed haven.

—Frances J. Roberts

A nature lover's modest home overlooks Wyman Lake near Bingham, Maine. Photo by Steve Terrill.

Song of Gray Things

Elizabeth-Ellen Long

In any weather, any day,
Much is lovely that is gray—
Driftwood smoothed to satin by
The tide's cool fingers, early sky,
Lichen stars that lightly dapple
Stone walls around an apple
Orchard, birch bark, and the thin
Warped rails of fences holding in
Reluctant meadows, kittens' fur,
Dried wild grasses sweet as myrrh,
As well as cobweb lace on eaves,
Sudden wind in willow leaves,
And pigeons proudly marching down
The slanted rooftops of a town.

A gray cat rests on a Kilim rug.
Photo by Jessie Walker.

THE DOG
(As Seen by the Cat)

Oliver Herford

The Dog is **BLACK** or *WHITE* or **BROWN**
And sometimes SPOTTED like a clown.
He loves to make a foolish noise,
And Human Company enjoys.

The Human People pat his head
And teach him to pretend he's dead,
And beg, and fetch, and carry, too;
Things that no well-bred Cat will do.

At Human jokes, however stale,
He JUMPS about and WAGS his tail,
And Human People clap their hands
And think he really understands.

They say "Good Dog" to him. To us
They say "Poor Puss" and make no fuss.
Why Dogs are "good" and Cats are "poor"
I fail to understand, I'm sure.

To Someone very Good and Just,
Who has proved worthy of her trust,
A Cat will sometimes condescend—
The dog is everybody's friend!

A boy finds his puppy to be the perfect pillow in BEST FRIENDS *by artist Donald Zolan. Image copyright © Pemberton & Oakes.*

THE *Children* IN Autumn

Daniel Whitehead Hicky

They are unconcerned with autumn now, the children
Playing beneath this sudden blazing of the maples.
Autumn might just as well have come, for all they notice,
To the Far Pacific's islands or the boulevards of Naples.

The reds and golds of autumn are joined by a boy and his kitty. Photo by Superstock.

Young brothers enjoy a day's worth of raked leaves in this photo by Scott Barrow/International Stock.

I hear them playing loudly under the reddening myrtles

The games they played when April captured the whitening park;

Their signals are all the same and their laughing playmates even,

But they do not see the embers of leaves that light the gathering dark.

Autumn is fast upon us, but not for the eyes of the children.

It is for us, their elders, who carry its name in our talk,

Who sensed it before the turning of a maple leaf or the sumac,

Before a scarlet cinder fell from the salvia's stalk.

MARBLES

Michael Paul Burgess

Knuckle down! On hearing those words, I leave my seventy-something self behind and am once again a boy of eight, slamming the screen door as I rush in to tell my parents the good news—my aggie had hit the mark, and I held the coveted title of marble champion of East Magnolia Street. My father offered a proud pat on the back and my mother congratulated me, albeit a bit tentatively (for she, like every good Sunday-school teacher, frowned upon playing marbles for keeps). I couldn't stop smiling, and I was glowing with victory, at least until the preacher's daughter claimed my title at the next afternoon's game.

In the mid 1930s and early 1940s, the sporting arena was the alley behind the schoolhouse, and the equipment of choice was a "cat's eye" or "immie." A junior-high sports star had no more respect than a proficient marble shooter with a calloused thumb knuckle and a horde of marbles to prove his or her talent. To an eight-year-old boy such as myself, marbles offered a magical world, a world filled with shiny spheres with such image-provoking names as flames, slags, oxbloods, and black widows.

I have always loved marbles. As long as I can remember, I kept a Quaker Oats box full of them beneath my bed. Some of my earliest memories are of grabbing my box and rushing to meet my friends in the dusty clearing behind Charlie Spencer's house. My mother notwithstanding, marbles were a family tradition. My father had a large collection from his own childhood, and he would offer comments on mine as I sorted them by type, color, and size. When their numbers seemed low, I would make my own "commoneys" from clay; or my father would give me a few cents to buy replacements at the local five-and-dime.

My prized marble was a gift from my father's own collection. It was a red, white, and blue peppermint swirl, first created in the 1870s to commemorate America's centennial celebration. I thought it looked pretty enough to eat, and I kept it with me always. When a teacher's questions caught me unprepared, I would shrug my shoulders and thrust my hands deep into the pockets of my jeans. There I would inevitably find my peppermint swirl marble and a few other small ones. I particularly remember their comforting smoothness on my fingertips and their familiar clank as they rattled against one other.

But I soon grew up, and my pockets were no longer filled with marbles, but with car keys and money clips. I set aside my marble collection for many years until my son was old enough to appreciate the game. Then it was as if I were eight again, showing my son how to choose a winning marble, how to hold his hand, and how to shoot to win. From that time on, I was hooked once again on those magical little spheres.

Using the contents of my oats box as a start, I began to rebuild my collection and search out the kinds of marbles I had dreamed of owning as a boy. At local marble shows, I traded with other forty-something marble enthusiasts who were revisiting a bit of their past as well. Since then, I have accumulated such treasures as open-core swirls, half-inch pee-wees, and clambroths with milky swirls of color.

My marble collection has now moved beyond the oats box to a special display cabinet. On the top shelf rests the peppermint swirl marble given to me by my father. Next to it is another favorite member of my collection: an Indian swirl splashed with brilliant colors. It was given to me by my adult son, proof that I aptly passed on my appreciation for the beauty and simplicity of marbles. I hope to continue the tradition and give a few of my marbles to my seven-year-old grandson. For now, he's still insisting on his need for the newest video game and in-line skates. As he pleads his case, I can't help but reminisce about a past day when a boy with only a pocketful of marbles felt like the king of the world.

PLAYING FOR KEEPS

If you would like to collect marbles, the following information will be helpful:

HISTORY

• Marbles made of clay or stone were used in games played by the ancient Egyptians, Greeks, and Romans. Some of these marbles survive today.

• In the nineteenth century, Germany was famous for its handmade stone marbles. Most German marble mills closed during the first World War.

• In the United States, marbles reached the height of their popularity between 1850 and 1890. The majority of the marbles were imported from Europe until the 1880s, when American companies first began manufacturing them.

• In 1903, Danish immigrant Martin Frederick Christensen began producing the first machine-made glass marbles at the rate of one thousand marbles per hour.

• During the 1950s, Japan flooded the American market with its popular cat's-eye marbles, which were unreproducible by American marblers for five years.

BUILDING A COLLECTION

• Marbles range in size from smaller than ½ inch to 2½ inches.

• Prices can range from fifty cents to more than $5,000 for a rare marble in pristine condition (no bruises, chips, dings, or cracks). Many highly collectible marbles can be found for less than $100.

• Generally, prices increase as size and amount of color increase. Handmade marbles are more valuable than the machine-made variety.

MARBLE MATERIALS

• Clay (earthenware, spatterware, salt-glazed)
• Stone (made from agate, rose quartz, or opal)
• Porcelain (often painted with designs, flowers, or scenes)
• Glass (can be either cane cut, individually crafted, or machine-made)
• Marble (sometimes called "taws" or "alleys")

A marble collection is displayed in a specially built cabinet. Photo by Jessie Walker.

SPECIAL FINDS

• Marbles known as end-of-days, which the glassblower created using the day's leftover pieces of glass.

• Sulfides, which are hand-blown marbles embedded with an animal or facial figure. Colored sulfides or those containing images of famous persons or characters are particularly valuable.

• Lutzes, which gleam with goldstone and are named for master craftsman Nicholas Lutz.

 Little Red Schoolhouse

Ruth Jenner

Once long ago a schoolhouse stood
Beneath tall trees of cottonwood;
A small school in a trampled yard
By years of childish footbeats scarred,
A fence, a stile, a wide-plank walk,
All marked for games with blackboard chalk.

A handbell with discordant din
Would summon straggling children in;
Reluctantly, with backward looks
They turned to learning gained from books—
Some lessons of a formal make
To add to those of "give and take."

In retrospect, I still recall
The corner stove, the windowed wall,
The board's expanse, dull black and wide,
With cloak-rooms ranged on either side,
And rows of desks for every grade,
Where future citizens were made.

The years have rapidly passed on—
The small red schoolhouse now is gone.
But since it was, it can but be
An instrument of destiny
To all whose memories still know
That little school of long ago.

*This schoolhouse, built in 1858, provided many a
lesson in Poland, Ohio. Photo by Gene Ahrens.*

WHATEVER HAPPENED TO RUN, SHEEP, RUN?

Marjorie Holmes

Whatever happened, I sometimes wonder, to hide-and-seek? And pump, pump, pull-away, as we called it. And Old Gray Wolf? And where, oh, where are the children who used to trample gardens, clamber over fences, and shatter the quiet darkness with their cries of "Run, sheep, run!" They're now suburban housewives like me, I suppose, or busy commuting dads. And their offspring are just as eager as we were to play out-of-doors after supper, and no doubt just as stricken by the stern, inevitable voices of parents calling them in. . . .

They dare not rove as we did, often for blocks and blocks in the dreamy security of our little town. And where in all suburbia would they find the wonderful places to hide? The woodsheds and gullies, the icehouse, the few remaining haymows, and all the enthralling nooks and crannies of the vast, deserted Chautauqua pavilion in the cool, tree-studded park.

The crowds began to gather right after supper, in that lovely twilight hour just before the street-lamps came on. . . . Little girls, with a final swipe at the sink or the kitchen floor, tore wildly out to join their brothers, already gravitated to the corner streetlight, focal point of almost all our games. . . . Once we all got together, the whole business of counting out and choosing sides had to be done. Only the meek and unimaginative fell back on the old familiar "Eenie-Meenie" method of counting out. Older, tougher hands came up with . . . "One potato, two potato, three potato, *four!*"

It having been determined, we'd all taunt, "Yer It, yer It, you've got a fit and don't know how to get out of it!" as he buried his face against the faithful lamppost and began to count. That was signal enough for us to tear off through the gathering dusk to hide. . . .

All our favorite games involved hiding and mystery and pursuit, culminating in a violent chase.

But the one that really sent us was Run, Sheep, Run. For this you chose up two sides, with a captain for each. One band would remain at the lamppost, while the other slipped away in search of some new, impregnable, totally unsuspected hiding place. Up alleys, across back fences, through vacant lots, back-tracking so as to leave no clues. . . .

Everybody wanted to be captain. The captain got to make up the signals and call them out importantly. If he were the phlegmatic sort he settled for dull, ordinary code words—like "catsup," or "onion stew." Others were wildly inventive, rhythmic, and often funny: "Now if I holler 'Baby ate the preacher' that'll mean don't worry, we're going the other direction. . . . 'Join the circus!' will mean here we come, get ready to run."

Plotting and conspiring, we huddled together in the finally chosen den—a culvert, Redenbaughs' woodpile, a cellar with slanting doors through which you could peek, a barn, a garage, behind the pillars of the yawning park pavilion. Then the captain would circle back to confront the enemy, crossing his index fingers to indicate the directions in which we might be. Taut, we listened for his first vital signal informing us of their choice. But we were not free to move until we heard his further alarms, warnings, and messages, no matter how far the foe might be led astray.

In a bliss of fear, suspense, anticipation, we waited, listening—listening. . . . Stars glittered overhead. Frogs thumped their deep bass fiddles in the rushes along the lake. Crickets and locusts chirped and racketed in the trees. Bats swooped low. A player piano poured its liquid music into the street. A slow freight rumbled through town. . . . There was the lonely barking of dogs. The whole night was strange, delicious with danger.

Signals dimmed the distance, or drew nearer. Shuddering, we clutched each other at the

The barn door provides a hiding spot for a few neighborhood friends. Photo by FPG International.

approaching footsteps, the voices speculating. Then at last the final signal, the glorious release. They had tracked us down or were hot on the trail: "Run, sheep, run!" Screaming like wild horses, we came tearing out of our hiding place, not sheep at all, but frantic creatures pounding madly home. For your goal, the sole center of your existence, was that serenely shining beacon on the distant corner, the pale and patient streetlamp. . . .

Now it was the other side's turn to hide. And it was almost as exciting to try to figure out their signals and trail them to their lair. Hot and sweaty from our run, we trudged the town, often in vehement argument with their leader, always alert to his tricks. Drinking great draughts of the night air, rich with its smell of clover and trampled grass and dirty kids. Wishing on falling stars. . . . And always, long before you had had enough, parental voices began calling you in. You heard them no matter how far you had ranged, or scouts announced your doom. "Hey, your mother's calling." . . .

It's nice to know there are a few pleasures that bridge the generations, that don't mystify and amuse my progeny when I speak of "bygone days." They think it sad and rather funny that we didn't have air conditioning and freezers and TV and space flights. They'll never understand the thrill of the space flights we took almost every night . . . up alleys, over fences, through gardens and yards and the starry park, playing Run, Sheep, Run!

OF SCHOOL AGE

Maude Woods Plessinger

She brushed his hair and pressed upon his brow
A kiss, then flicked a raveling from his coat.
Bye, bye, she waved, but something in her throat
Shut off the words, and vision failed her now
As hesitatingly he went and then
She saw him swallowed up among the youth
Enroute to school and realized the truth—

That he would never be the same again.
But she would always have the memory
Of love-filled days, his darling babyhood.
And if he only grew up to be good,
Then facing her responsibility
She looked out bravely through a well of tears
And prayed for guidance through the coming years.

A school day of yesteryear is pictured in THE COUNTRY SCHOOL *by artist Homer Winslow. Image from City Art Museum of St. Louis/Superstock.*

SCHOOL BEGINS

Eleanor Graham Vance

With summer tan aglow on freckled faces,
With hands scrubbed clean that were (and will be) black,
They tumble in and take their schoolroom places,
Half eager, half reluctant to be back.
I meet them in my best schoolteacher fashion,
I let them ramble on about their fun,
Then try to make them work with that same passion

They always give to playing in the sun.
Outside the summer melts in autumn haze,
A locust drones his homage to the light,
A warm breeze blows across the meadow-ways;
The children's wistful eyes are misty-bright.
And while their gaze is fixed beyond the door,
I have to teach them two and two are four!

OUR HERITAGE

ON THE EDUCATION OF YOUTH IN AMERICA

Noah Webster, 1788

Every child in America should be acquainted with his own country. He should read books that furnish him with ideas that will be useful to him in life and practice. As soon as he opens his lips, he should rehearse the history of his own country; he should lisp the praise of liberty, and of those illustrious heroes and statesmen who have wrought a revolution in her favor. . . .

When I speak of the diffusion of knowledge, I do not mean merely a knowledge of spelling books, and the New Testament. An acquaintance with ethics, and with the general principles of law, commerce, money and government, is necessary for the yeomanry of a republican state. This acquaintance they might obtain by means of books calculated for schools, and read by the children, during the winter months, and by the circulation of public papers. . . .

Every small district should be furnished with a school, at least four months in a year. . . . This school should be kept by the most reputable and well informed man in the district. Here children should be taught the usual branches of learning; submission to superiors and to laws; the moral or social duties; the history and transactions of their own country;

the principles of liberty and government. Here the rough manners of the wilderness should be softened, and the principles of virtue and good behaviours inculcated. The *virtues* of men are of more consequence to society than their *abilities*; and for this reason, the *heart* should be cultivated with more assiduity than the *head*.

Such a general system of education is neither impracticable nor difficult; and expecting the formation of a federal government that shall be efficient and permanent, it demands the first attention of American patriots. Until such a system shall be adopted and pursued; until the Statesman and Divine shall unite their efforts in *forming* the human mind, rather than in loping its excrescences, after it has been neglected; until Legislators discover that the only way to make good citizens and subjects is to nourish them from infancy; and until parents shall be convinced that the *worst* of men are not the proper teachers to make the *best*; mankind cannot know to what a degree of perfection society and government may be carried. America affords the fairest opportunities for making the experiment, and opens the most encouraging prospect of success.

ABOUT THE TEXT

In the late eighteenth century, Noah Webster, a lawyer, teacher, and author of such educational boons as the Blue-Backed Speller, was one of the earliest proponents of educational reform in America. At the time, the country was only beginning to develop its intellectual and social structures, and Webster recognized the young nation's need for civic education to create a sense of national spirit and unity. It was dedication such as his that established America's educational system, a system now enjoyed by millions of schoolchildren across the nation.

Noah Webster's childhood home still stands in West Hartford, Connecticut. Photo courtesy The Noah Webster House.

NOAH WEBSTER

Writers of dictionaries are not often counted among a nation's heroes. Such honors are generally reserved for soldiers and statesmen, explorers and scientists. Certainly not lexographers. Aren't they, after all, merely recorders and compilers of the language they read and hear around them? What is heroic in that? Such is the fate of Noah Webster, an American known widely by name as the author of a dictionary, but given little further consideration; an American who had the misfortune to be counted as a cold and difficult man in his day and who thereafter has been relegated to the trivia question category of America's history game.

Noah Webster was born in West Hartford, Connecticut, in 1758. He was raised in a family of farmers; but from the very beginning, young Noah favored books and learning over plows and crops. Still, although he was clearly of an intellectual bent, Webster had trouble deciding what to do with this inclination. He studied at Yale and then went on to teach. Dissatisfied, he studied law only to decide against working as an attorney. He then returned to teaching and found it just as unsatisfactory as before.

Webster seemed to be falling short of his potential

until 1785, when he came upon an idea that would finally give direction to his faltering career. He published a speller for schoolchildren that was called *The American Spelling Book*. Webster was determined to set a universal standard of spelling and usage for America's schoolchildren, and he went on a one-man crusade to promote the book. Soon the *Blue-Backed Speller*, as it was commonly known, was in the hands of schoolchildren from Webster's native New England to the far western reaches of the frontier settlements. "A national language," he wrote, "is a bond of national union." Webster used moral stories and patriotic tales to teach both reading and spelling, and his grand visions for his speller were not far from actuality. By the year 1900, seventy-five million copies of his book had been sold, making it the second most popular book in America after the Bible.

Behind Noah Webster's speller was a patriotism that had been born with the nation. He had twice abandoned his studies at Yale to fight in the colonial militia, and after the battle for independence he had written and spoken frequently in support of the Revolution. At the time he produced his speller, Webster fervently believed in the democratic beliefs upon which the nation had been founded. He was convinced that America was an experiment that would prove the unlimited potential of man to perfect himself and his society.

In 1800, Webster channeled his energies into a new project—the *American Dictionary of the English Language*. The work was a massive undertaking: seventy thousand entries written by his own hand to give Americans a standard of spelling, pronunciation, and meaning for their language. For a quarter of a century, Noah Webster devoted himself fully to the task of completing this dictionary; it was his gift to the nation he loved.

Webster's dictionary was a monumental achievement. Its very existence was a declaration that American English was as important as British English, an idea not readily accepted across the Atlantic. The dictionary also openly acknowledged, by its inclusion of new words and new definitions, that language was a living, evolving thing—an idea that many old-school linguists adamantly opposed. Webster's dictionary became the American standard, and his name eventually became synonymous with the genre.

Paired with his speller, the dictionary gave Americans the language to understand each other even as they spread across the continent. It gave Californians the same definition for a word as Vermonters. It helped to prevent the division of our language into regional dialects indecipherable to one another. Given the rapid pace and the enormous scope of American expansion during the 1800s, it is truly miraculous that the nation remained of one piece. Noah Webster played no small role in that miracle.

Yet throughout history, Webster has received little recognition for his work, beginning in his general lack of popularity during his own day. Reading his biography, one gets the picture of Webster as the perpetual outsider, someone who, at a momentous time in American history, was often on the scene but never in the limelight. He counted George Washington, Thomas Jefferson, and Benjamin Franklin among his acquaintances, but few men or women among his friends. One contemporary described Webster as "cold, cantankerous, authoritative, and self-righteous." Another recorded that "in conversation," Webster was "even duller than in writing." Even Webster himself seemed to concur, writing, "I suspect I am not formed for society."

Upon any inquiry into the life of Noah Webster, however, it quickly becomes apparent that even though his public reputation was that of a difficult, egocentric man, he had a warm-hearted side that his family knew well. A devoted husband, a loving and playful father and grandfather, Webster knew great contentment in his private life.

Noah Webster presented his dictionary to his fellow Americans with the hope that it would provide some stability and unity in a tumultuous age; undoubtedly he also must have hoped for some measure of notoriety for his great achievement. He reached his first goal, but fell short of the acclaim of which he may have dreamed. Noah Webster was not forgotten by history, but he was unfairly neglected and marginalized. Any honest accounting should label Webster a hero, and one worthy of respect and emulation; for his contribution to our national story required neither sword nor firearm nor the power of high office. All that Noah Webster needed was twenty-five years of painstaking work and the knowledge that language has the power to shape a nation.

MY OLD FRIEND

James Whitcomb Riley

You've a manner all so mellow,
    My old friend,
That it cheers and warms a fellow,
    My old friend,
Just to meet and greet you, and
Feel the pressure of a hand
That one may understand,
    My old friend.

Though dimmed in youthful splendor,
    My old friend,
Your smiles are still as tender,
    My old friend,
And your eyes as true a blue
As your childhood ever knew,
And your laugh as merry, too,
    My old friend.

For though your hair is faded,
    My old friend,
And your step a trifle jaded,
    My old friend,
Old Time, with all his lures
In the trophies he secures,
Leaves young that heart of yours,
    My old friend.

And so it is you cheer me,
    My old friend,
For to know you still are near me,
    My old friend,
Makes my hope of clearer light,
And my faith of surer sight,
And my soul a purer white,
    My old friend.

*Two friends share a day of paddling and chatting in
Harrison, Maine. Photo by Dianne Dietrich Leis.*

TRAVELER'S Diary

THE LIBRARY OF CONGRESS, WASHINGTON, D.C.

Nora J. Smithson

I first visited the Library of Congress as a young girl on a trip to Washington, D.C., with my parents. The library was just one stop on a whirlwind two-day tour of the capital, and I must admit that I remember very little, except for the enormous dome above the main reading room of the Jefferson Building. What I do remember is that my parents were impressed, even awed by the library and its collections. They tried to pique my interest in the place by speaking in serious tones about the importance of books and libraries and education. I don't recall placing too much weight on their words at the time, but I remember them all these years later, so they obviously made some impression.

Last summer, I revisited the Library of Congress, more than twenty years later. And I brought my own young daughters. This time, it was their turn to stare in wonder at the giant dome—which rises seventy-five feet to a stained glass ceiling—and my turn to be awed by this remarkable American treasure.

The Library of Congress, which should more accurately be called the "Library of America," began as a collection of 152 volumes to aid the members of Congress in researching bills. That was in the year 1800. The fact that the library grew to its modern size—which includes more than one hundred million books, manuscripts, maps, photographs, recordings, prints, and other pieces—is due to the vision of Thomas Jefferson. During the eight years of his presidency, and throughout his lifetime thereafter, Jefferson took a personal interest in building the library. He signed laws that defined a purpose and scope for the library beyond Congressional use, and he created the position of Librarian of Congress, thereby assuring that the library would always have an official guardian. Jefferson's devotion to the library grew out of his lifelong belief that the key to a stable democracy was an educated populous. In 1815, the former president sold his personal collection of 6,500 volumes to the government, assuring that the Library of Congress collection would not remain an eclectic collection for the use of lawmakers but would become a diverse collection for the nation as a whole.

When the library opened in 1800, the collections were housed inside a Washington boardinghouse. Later, the books and materials were moved to the Capitol. In 1897, the Thomas Jefferson Building was opened. The John Adams Building was added in 1939, and the James Madison Memorial Building completed the modern library in 1980. The Jefferson Building, which was recently renovated, is the most impressive of the three; its dome is breathtaking, and I was thrilled with the collection of paintings and sculptures by American artists that fill the main reading room.

The Library of Congress today serves its original purpose as a research facility for Congress but also serves common American citizens, researchers, and scholars. It is the largest library in the world. And the collections are still growing, at the astounding rate of seven thousand items per day (every book copyrighted in America is sent to the Library).

In literature my daughters and I picked up on our tour of the library, its modern purpose is stated as creating a "comprehensive record of American history and creativity and a universal collection of human knowledge." The Library of Congress is as wonderful as its goals are lofty. I'm glad I revisited the library and glad I introduced my children to it. My parents, like Jefferson before them, were right. Books and learning and libraries are essential, and there is no greater monument to their value than the Library of Congress.

The main reading room at the Library of Congress, photographed by Stan Ries/International Stock.

Fiftieth Reunion

Joyce S. Anderson

I have never returned to a college or high school reunion. Call it the Thomas Wolfe you-can't-go-home-again syndrome. I prefer to keep the past safe, intact, and neatly encased in a nostalgic cardboard box where it belongs. But a few autumns ago, with a cooperative if somewhat skeptical spouse in tow, I was there at the fiftieth reunion of Paterson Eastside High School, class of 1947. So why the switch?

In early September, an intriguing message spoke out from our telephone answering machine. "If this is Joyce Sloan Anderson from E.H.S. in Paterson, please call me. We're having a fiftieth reunion, and you've been on the 'lost' list until today." With the caller's name and phone number, I then searched for my yearbook (no small achievement) to look up her picture before I returned the call.

There was her face at eighteen, swimming up through the decades, head of the cap-and-gown committee and still apparently active in keeping the class spirit alive. In a senior class of more than two hundred students, we had all known each other. I called her right away.

"We've been working on this for a year and a half," she told me after our initial exchanges. "You were missing along with many other women whose married names we didn't have and some of the men too."

"How did you find me?" I queried.

"Well, someone knew a friend of your sister. We called the friend, and he gave us her married name. Then we called your sister, and that did it."

"And who was the someone?" I asked.

Her answer identified my high-school boyfriend, the closest to a "steady" in those days. We dated on and off throughout our four years at Eastside; the final event being a disastrous fight at the senior prom. I remember spending half the night in the ladies' room of the Crown Court Hall in New York. The ladies' room was where we went in those years to be consoled by our girlfriends when things went wrong at a dance. Looking back fifty years, it all seemed too hilarious! I decided to go, and the next morning I called back my former classmate.

"Is there going to be a booklet? With write-ups about each person?"

"Yes, Joyce, but it went to press last week. Sorry."

"Am I going to be the only one there who won't be in the booklet?"

"Yes," she replied.

"Well," I said, "How about my writing up a summary? I'll make copies and stuff the booklets before the others arrive."

"Fine."

I certainly wasn't going to be the only one without a past. A five-decade cipher! She sent me the questionnaire as a guide, and I noted that there were four lines to answer the question *What have you been doing since 1947?* My mind usually goes blank when people ask me what I did last summer or last weekend. Now I had only one paragraph to summarize my entire adult life. I was tempted to start with Nobel Prize (only kidding), but thought better of that approach and played it straight.

The major decision looming ahead was what to wear. I usually opt for a classic outfit and was considering the black-and-white checked jacket over black cashmere sweater and skirt. The trio of my daughter, sister, and hairdresser unanimously turned thumbs down on that idea. In fact, they were vehemently opposed. Daughter, "You want to look smashing!" Sister, "They already know

you're smart." (I ranked in the top ten of the class.) Hairdresser, "You'll look like a college professor." (Of course, that was what I was, but the facts were beside the point in that discussion.) With total approval from my three fashion consultants, I opted for the Chinese red suit with appropriate understatedly elegant accessories. No shrinking alumna, I.

The list of attendees arrived, and I was happy to see the names of some of my closest friends during my school years. I called Adele in Arizona, and we caught up on five decades of living. She too had moved away and had been completely out of touch. I was looking forward to

seeing her, my erstwhile boyfriend, and other time travelers. I was ready.

The day after the reunion, I realized that Thomas Wolfe was wrong after all. I had one of the best times of my life. The classmates were warm and embracing. The ex-boyfriend and I danced, and neither of us could remember why we had the big fight at the senior prom. Even my husband enjoyed his role as spectator spouse. All in all, my fiftieth reunion turned out to be a life-affirming experience for me, as well as an emotional high. With the 1940s music in the background, the years fell away; and for one lovely night, I felt like seventeen again.

HANDMADE HEIRLOOM

◆◆◆

A framed reunion invitation is surrounded by other memories of high school.

REUNION INVITATION IN CALLIGRAPHY

Michelle Prater Burke

A long-standing joke between my friends and me is that I never could have been a doctor because my handwriting is too neat. It has been that way since the fourth grade, when my teacher, Mrs. Davis, first taught me to write in cursive. I felt like quite the grown-up as I carefully connected each curly letter to the next, stretching my lowercase "A" precisely to the dotted line and adding that perfect little tail to the capital "T." Learning to write cursive was almost like an art class to me, and I spent the following summer sitting on my front porch, doodling my name over and over again and trying to create the perfect signature.

My practice must have paid off, because from that year on I became "the one with the pretty handwriting" to all my friends and, eventually, coworkers. Anytime there was a certificate to be filled out, I was called. Greeting card, bookplate, placecard—they all became my responsibility. To friends of mine whose penmanship is illegible, I am the answer whenever handwriting counts. Perhaps it was this unofficial post as designated handwriter that led me to take a class in calligraphy.

The word calligraphy comes from the Greek word *kallos*, meaning beauty, and *graphe*, meaning writing. The art of writing beautifully is ancient, developed centuries ago by diligent scribes working on animal skins with quills that were hardened and cut to size by hand. Most of the letterforms used today are derived from such timeless originals as the precise capitals used in ancient Rome or the graceful italic hand developed by fifteenth- and sixteenth-century Renaissance scribes.

In 1898, a British calligrapher named Edward Johnston began researching such early examples of handwriting in the British Museum's manuscript collection. He was excited by what he found and passed on his enthusiasm to his calligraphy students at London's Central School of Arts and Crafts. It was Johnston's interest in ancient calligraphy that revived the art of writing with a broad-edged tool and reshaped it into a skill for the twentieth century.

Today, calligraphy offers modern writers a link to a slower age when handwritten notes were the norm. The beautiful script used by ancient men of letters can be learned by anyone willing to train his or her eye and hand through practice. Calligraphy experts suggest an hour of practice each day to create consistent results. Although that sort of time dedication may be unreachable, a small amount of practice and patience can give you a good start on your first project. And once you begin writing, you are likely to find more and more reasons to practice and learn.

As your calligraphy skills develop and your friends hear of it, be prepared to ply your pen often. A few months ago, my friend Pat was planning her fortieth high-school reunion and asked me to create an invitation. Since it was such an important event, she wanted something that was suitable for framing.

I began the project by choosing several books on calligraphy from the library to inspire me. If you are not able to take a calligraphy class, these books offer step-by-step instructions and many projects. I used one to help me decide on a pleasing layout, create an initial paste-up, and choose the proper ink, nib, and paper. I decided to put the details of the reunion inside the invitation and reserve the outside for framing. After much experimentation, I chose two different lettering styles and created a large monogram from the name of the high school. The final product may not have been as perfect as that of a master calligrapher, but I was pleased; and Pat greatly appreciated my help in adding elegance to her special night.

Although I have much to learn about calligraphy, I continue to receive requests from my "penmanship challenged" friends. I've helped more than one bride-to-be with wedding invitations, and most recently I was asked to write the dedication page in a family Bible. Yet as I settle into my favorite chair with a pen full of ink and a new pad of paper, I realize that my real interest in calligraphy is purely selfish. A younger I once thrilled at the thought of learning a new and beautiful way to write letters, and calligraphy has allowed me to recapture that feeling. As I doodle and experiment, I become lost in the rhythmic flow of the ink and the flourishes that appear. If I'm not sure what to write, I always practice my name. After all, I'm still working on that perfect signature.

A Cup of Tea

Author Unknown

Nellie made a cup of tea,
Made and poured it out for me,
And above the steaming brew
Smiled and asked me, "One or two?"
Saucily she tossed her head;
"Make it sweet for me," I said.

Two sweet lumps of sugar fell
Into that small china well,
But I knew the while I drained
Every drop the cup contained,
More than sugar in the tea
Made the beverage sweet for me.

This to her I tried to say
In that golden yesterday—
Life is like a cup of tea

Which Time poureth endlessly,
Brewed by trial's constant heat,
Needing love to make it sweet.

Then I caught her looking up,
And I held my dainty cup
Out to her and bravely said,
"Here is all that lies ahead;
Here is all my life to be—
Will you make it sweet for me?"

That was years ago, and now
There is silver in her brow.
We have sorrowed, we have smiled.
We've been hurt and reconciled,
But whatever had to be,
She has made it sweet for me.

We cannot tell the precise moment when a friendship is formed. As in filling a vessel drop by drop, there is at last a drop which makes it run over; so in a series of kindnesses there is at last one which makes the heart run over. —*Samuel Johnson*

A teapot becomes a charming vase for a bouquet of pansies. Photo by Nancy Matthews.

The Quiet Friendship

Grace V. Watkins

Friendship of old men is a quiet thing,
Textured of memory and faith unspoken.
Winter and summer mornings dawn and wing
Into the past without a sign or token.

When two old men sit on the porch together,
Watching the shadows of the evening thicken,
Exchanging scattered words about the weather,
They feel a silence as the night winds quicken.

One of them left alone will show no trace
Of grief nor walk across the bridge that lies
Between the small town and the burying place,
Yet sometimes an old man will feel his eyes
Fill with quick tears if he should chance to meet
An old friend's son along the village street.

Artist Deidre Scherer's unique talent is demonstrated in her touching fabric-and-thread work entitled FRAGMENTS. *Image from the book* THREADS OF EXPERIENCE, *published by Papier-Mache Press. Photo by Jeff Baird.*

Readers' Reflections

Editor's Note: Readers are invited to submit unpublished, original poetry for possible publication in future issues of Ideals. *Please send typed copies only; manuscripts will not be returned. Writers receive $10 for each published submission. Send material to Readers' Reflections, Ideals Publications Inc., P.O. Box 305300, Nashville, Tennessee 37230-5300.*

Another Day
Judie Harding
Waverly, Pennsylvania

The joy of yet another day
To work, to play, or while away,
To feel the warmth of sun on high,
To watch while lofty clouds drift by,
To gaze upon the verdant land,
To see the mighty forest stand,
To gather moss along the stream,
To rest and take the time to dream,
To pick a rosebud fresh with dew,
To know each day will start anew,
To smell the sweetness in the air,
To have someone with whom to share,
To capture moonbeams from the sky,
To hum a tune from years gone by,
To dance with fairies from afar,
To make one wish upon a star,
To love, to laugh, to hope, to pray,
To know the joy of yet another day.

Echoes of My Mind
Brenda Johnson
Mountain Home, Arkansas

The echoes of my childhood
Call out in memories.
And bring back friends of yesterday
That I long to see.
In the crowded hallways of my mind,
We linger after school,
Or drink old-fashioned sodas
Atop soda-fountain stools.
Ballgames are played, sock hops are danced;
My but those were the days!
When car hops worked on roller skates
And jukeboxes were the craze.
How I miss those days of old
When friends were genuine.
Yet I still have them here with me,
In the echoes of my mind.

Snapshots

Martha Mastin
Walls, Mississippi

Some folks have family albums
With pictures neat and nice.
For us the tattered shoeboxes
Still seem to quite suffice.
Old snapshots shared with loved ones
Bring back fond memories
Of "Good Ole Days" when we were young
"Hold still! Now smile! Say cheese."
These treasures in a shoebox
Are dog-eared, cracked, and old;
But childhood memories relived
Are worth their wait in gold.

A Friend

Carolyn Kimzey
Hendersonville, North Carolina

You came by today,
Bracing as a cooling breeze;
Like the fresh water pouring
From a freely gushing spring.

Soon I was refreshed;
Lifting my head, I could see
Things not seen before—
Mellow autumn leaves, and swift
Sudden curve of bluebird's wing.

Prayer for a Friend

Evelyn Kintop
Leesburg, Florida

Let me be worthy to love thee, friend,
    as purely as I should
With the strength of my devotion
    inspiring me to good.
Let me serve thee in the menial tasks
    that others deem too small,
Striving in my efforts
    to please thee most of all.
Let me learn to step aside, dear friend,
    should others have a need,
Relinquishing possessiveness,
    resisting selfish greed,

Knowing well the ties that bind us
    are too strong to break apart
As I cling to tender memories
    from the garden of my heart.
Let my love be not demanding
    but rather let it be
Like a rainbow on thy pathway
    ever leading back to me,
Full of golden dreams and laughter,
    ever faithful to the end;
Oh, teach me how to love thee
    and be worthy of thee, friend.

Faith's Octave

Alice Kennelly Roberts

Dogging my footsteps are eight little paws,
Governed by faith and devotion's great laws,
Four for a terrier, foxy and white,
Four for a collie, now losing her sight;

Whether at typewriter, table, or den,
Going to bed or arising again,
Always the eight little paws find the way,
Whether in morning or late in the day;

Whether a closed door has barred them
from sight,
Whether the darkness has brought
on the night,
Softly and quietly, they are at hand,
Saying quite silently, "We understand."

Thus it has been for
the last fourteen years,
Thus it will be till for them
death appears.
What man could learn
about serving a cause—
Faith and devotion
in eight little paws!

Faithful friends meet in THE MORNING GREETING *by artist Arthur John Elsley. Image from Christie's Images, New York/Superstock.*

Some Small Delight

Milly Walton

Give me this day some small delight,
Some simple joy to cheer my soul,
A singing bird upon the bough,
A drifting cloud in sky's blue bowl;
The pealing laughter of my child,
The glint of sunlight on his hair,
The feel of his warm hand in mine,
Of these dear things make me aware;
A blossom in the garden spot,
The music of the poplar trees,
The fragrance of a dew-washed earth,
What could enchant me more than these?
Grant me perception that I may
Live deeply through this chartless day,
And when I go to sleep tonight
Be thankful for each small delight.

Several goldfinches and a cardinal share a meal in Missouri. Photo by Gay Bumgarner.

Rainbow Rain

Tom McFadden

Once on a twilight, solo stroll

Among the culminating hues,

I opened my mind for the private thrills

With which an autumn wood imbues.

Suddenly, in solitary spot,

Deep within one brilliant patch,

A potent wind, in quick surprise,

Rushed through full limbs to thus detach

The leaves, which fell so thickly down

On me, as in an autumn game,

Staying long in soft descent,

Thrilling me in rainbow rain.

Maple leaves and blue elderberries float along the Alsea River in Oregon. Photo by Dennis Frates.

A SLICE OF LIFE

Edgar A. Guest

THE APPLE TREE

When an apple tree is ready for the world
    to come and eat,
There isn't any structure in the land
    that's got it beat.
There's nothing man has builded
    with the beauty or the charm
That can touch the simple grandeur
    of the monarch of the farm.
There's never any picture
    from a human being's brush
That has ever caught the redness
    of a single apple's blush.

When an apple tree's in blossom
    it is glorious to see,
But that's just a hint, at springtime,
    of the better things to be;
That is just a fairy promise
    from the Great Magician's wand

Of the wonders and the splendors
    that are waiting just beyond
The distant edge of summer;
    just a forecast of the treat
When the apple tree is ready for the world
    to come and eat.

Architects of splendid vision long have labored
    on the earth,
And have raised their dreams in marble
    and we've marveled at their worth;
Long the spires of costly churches have looked
    upward at the sky;
Rich in promise and in the beauty,
    they have cheered the passer-by.
But I'm sure there's nothing finer
    for the eye of man to meet
Than an apple tree that's ready for the world
    to come and eat.

There's the promise of the apples,
    red and gleaming in the sun,
Like the medals worn by mortals
    as rewards for labors done;
And the big arms stretched wide open,
    with a welcome warm and true
In a way that sets you thinking
    it's intended just for you.
There is nothing with a beauty
    so entrancing, so complete,
As an apple tree that's ready
    for the world to come and eat.

Edgar A. Guest began his illustrious career in 1895 at the age of fourteen when his work first appeared in the Detroit Free Press. His column was syndicated in over three hundred newspapers, and he became known as "The Poet of the People."

Gifts of Autumn

Beverly J. Anderson

Autumn brings us misty mornings
With a crispness in the air,
Sapphire blue skies shining brightly,
And a brilliance everywhere.

Autumn brings us painted hillsides
With their foliage all ablaze—
Reds and yellow, scarlet, amber
Set against a purple haze.

Autumn brings us crimson maples,
Aspens that are gowned in gold,

Evergreens that lend their color—
All a beauty to behold!

Autumn brings us mums and asters,
Goldenrod and cattails tall,
Frosty evenings, warmth of fireside,
Full moon that gold-glimmers all.

Autumn brings us fruitful harvest,
Lavish bounty of the land,
Blessings with each day unfolding—
Gifts from God's all gracious hand.

Autumn Joys

Virginia Borman Grimmer

Oh, hear the rustling poplar trees,
Feel autumn's tantalizing breeze,
See the yonder hillside slope
With sassafras kaleidoscope.
Taste the purple grape so sweet
And savor long an apple treat.
Listen to the raucous geese
Giving up their northern lease,

Smell the pungency of mums,
Gather baskets full of plums.
Tie and save some herbs and dill,
Put a gourd upon the sill.
Bring the harvest bounty in,
Stock and pile each storage bin.
Just enjoy the great mystique
Of wondrous autumn, so unique.

*Prairie grasses, chrysanthemums, and a birdbath create an autumn
vignette in Bureau County, Illinois. Photo by Mary Liz Austin.*

From My Garden Journal

Deana Deck

APPLES

The first tree I ever climbed was a vigorous apple tree in my grandfather's backyard. At the time, my best friends were my two cousins, Karl Lee and Johnny. We were all the same age, born just months apart. As a result, we grew up like the Three Musketeers; wherever one led, the others followed. Climbing the tree seemed quite logical; we were hungry, and the lower branches were usually picked clean. Luckily, the tree was large enough to support the weight of three second-graders but small enough to have limbs one could jump or fall from without disastrous consequences. Of course we felt honor-bound to demonstrate our jumping abilities to each other, leaping from ever-higher limbs until one of us was wounded in action, and my grandfather temporarily banned us from climbing.

My grandfather's tree bore abundant apples, of what type I do not know. To a seven-year-old, all apples are the same, and the notion of varieties never seemed important. Our grandfather, known as Papoo in the family, was a farmer to his bones and planted the trees so long ago even he could not remember the type of apple the trees bore.

Papoo instilled in us an appreciation for all growing things, especially fruit trees. He would sit in his great big armchair by the console radio, and we three cousins would pile on top, vying for a spot on his lap. There we would practice reading. Instead of *Dick and Jane*, however, we read through the garden catalogs, especially those with pictures of luscious apples, pears, and peaches on the covers. It made our mouths water, and a catalog session often ended with a special treat—"wagon wheels."

Wagon wheels were slices of apple that Papoo cut with his large pocket knife after he had peeled and cored them. While we munched on our snacks, Karl Lee and Johnny and I would eagerly grab a piece of the discarded peel and toss it over our shoulders. The letter shape the peel formed on the floor was supposed to indicate the first initial of the person you were destined to marry someday. To a young girl, the game was quite exciting!

Unfortunately, some growing seasons weren't as successful as others, and the apples on my grandfather's tree would sometimes stay perpetually green. Because he never sprayed them, many fruits would be destroyed by hungry worms before they ripened. But during the years when the fruit did mature, the apples were the best I had ever put in my mouth.

Many years later, I lived in an apple-growing region of New York's Hudson Valley. There I learned that there are more apple varieties than I had ever imagined. About eight thousand varieties of apples are known worldwide. However, due to the advent of huge commercial orchards that plant on the greatest-common-denominator theory, only about one hundred varieties are grown in commercial quantity in the United States. Ninety percent is made up of only the top ten varieties. The result is that most supermarkets carry only three or four varieties of apples: Red or Yellow Delicious, Granny Smith, Winesaps or McIntosh, and sometimes Rome Beauty.

Today, if you want to savor some of the most unique and flavorful apples from generations past, you have to visit orchard country, where local farmers sell their crops from roadside stands. After you discover such taste-tempting varieties as the Gravenstein, Northern Spy, Starking, or Yellow Bellflower, your favorite apple-pie recipe will never be the same.

Although an orchard is out of the question, having an apple tree of my own would be lovely. Luckily, many dwarf and semi-dwarf varieties have been developed that solve the space problem presented by standard varieties. You can now grow an apple tree in the tiniest backyard or in the patio area of a condominium. All you need is sunshine.

The dwarf varieties are the smallest, maturing at just eight to ten feet in height. The semi-dwarf reaches ten to fifteen feet at maturity, but it yields standard-sized fruit. Most commercially available varieties can be obtained as dwarfs, including McIntosh, Granny Smith, and Red or Yellow Delicious, but some of the more uncommon varieties are available too through catalogs.

One new twist in apple growing is the increasingly popular pole or column form. These varieties can be grown in containers and reach eight feet in height but only two feet in width. They also bear standard-sized apples.

Since most apples require cross-pollination in order to produce fruit, at least two varieties must be planted. Even varieties that do not require cross-pollination produce more abundant crops when cross-pollinated by another variety. (Because pollination is so vital to fruit production, remember never to spray your tree when it's in blossom and attracting bees.)

Most apple trees require some cool winter weather, but there are varieties that are extremely cold hardy for northern gardens and others that tolerate the mild winters and hot summers of the south. The Haralson, for example, is one of the hardiest apples, capable of surviving sub-zero cold with no problem. A number of varieties will do well in climates as far south as Zone 8; and Granny Smith thrives even in Zone 9, which includes Central Florida, the Gulf Coast, and some of Southern California.

This wide choice of apple trees means that Karl Lee, Johnny, and I could find a variety of apple that is perfect for where each of us now lives: one in California, one in upstate New York, and one in Middle Tennessee. No matter how far apart we cousins are, we remain close friends, if no longer constant companions. And we will always share the memories of Papoo's apple tree, his delicious wagon wheels, and the days when we three were the apples of his eye!

Deana Deck tends to her flowers, plants, and vegetables at her home in Nashville, Tennessee, where her popular garden column is a regular feature in *The Tennessean*.

To the Goldenrod

Alice Kennelly Roberts

Thou tiny spark amid the green
That bearest still the sunlight's sheen,
That, glowing near the pasture rail,
Gives all the field a golden veil.

Thou comest not when daffodils
Blow lightly over Bluegrass hills,
Or honeysuckle, climbing high,
Reveals a longing for the sky.

Thou waitest till September's chill
Has touched the valley and the hill,
Till trees forsake their summer hue
And autumn paints the world anew.

Then doth thy lamp of lucent flame
Illumine earth from where thou came,
Gold—gold—as if thy tiny heart
Contained of every sun a part.

I would that thus beside life's road
Some traveller, bent beneath his load,
Might glimpse, like thine own taper lit,
My life to brighten earth a bit.

Unheralded

Lillie D. Chaffin

Unheralded, in sweeping tides,
The court of goldenrod arrives.
Along the roadsides, up the lanes,
It conquers land, then lays claim
To vases, jugs and windowsills.
Full flowering as it spills
Into the heart, takes full command
When crowning a small child's hand.

A field of goldenrod spreads below Big Jay and Little Jay Peaks in Montgomery, Vermont. Photo by William Johnson/Johnson's Photography.

Sacrament of Solitude

Jessie Wilmore Murton

Let us go far away from manmade things,
Beyond the reach of every fretful cry,
And look upon the miracle of wings,
Glory of autumn trees, and burnished sky.

The fragile aster, with its wondering orb
Of blue, uplifted bravely to the frost,
Shall be a star of hope against the drab
Of dull gray twilights, when the way seems lost.

And bittersweet, in scarlet clusters hung
Upon some ancient wall of crumbling stone,
Shall flame, banner of high courage flung
To winter's challenge, that we make our own.

Here we shall find a moment's respite where
No manmade touch may mar, no voice intrude,
And, shrived of all our little irking care,
Drink deep God's sacrament of solitude.

A hilltop offers a view of a patchwork of autumn color in Porcupine Mountains Wilderness State Park in Michigan. Photo by Carr Clifton.

Readers' Forum

Snapshots from Our Ideals Readers

Above: Two-and-a-half-year-old twin sisters Jennifer and Julie Leonard take time out for a kiss after making a card for their daddy. The snapshot was sent to us by the girls' grandmother, Doris Leonard of Cherry Hill, New Jersey. Doris says that although the twins are as different as night and day, they are constant companions.

Left: Six-month-old Bailey Hammett of Memphis, Tennessee, can't take her eyes off her best buddy, the family dog. The snapshot was sent to us by Bailey's great-grandmother, Mrs. Lorna M. Kavelman of Lincoln, Illinois.

Opposite top: Bob and Ethel Bryeans of Poplar Grove, Illinois, sent us this picture of their three granddaughters: Laura Pollard (age five), Natalie Bryeans (age five), and Ashley Bryeans (age three). The three cousins looked charming as they shared flower-girl responsibilities at a friend's fall wedding.

Opposite bottom: Mrs. Walter Davis of North Manchester, Indiana, couldn't be more proud of her two great-grandchildren, Levi and Alexsandra Davis. Mrs. Davis says the brother and sister, who live in Wausau, Wisconsin, are as close in person as they are in the picture.

THANK YOU Doris Leonard, Mrs. Lorna M. Kavelman, Bob and Ethel Bryeans, and Mrs. Walter Davis for sharing your family photographs with *Ideals*. We hope to hear from other readers who would like to share snapshots with the *Ideals* family. Please include a self-addressed, stamped envelope if you would like the photos returned. Keep your original photographs for safekeeping and send duplicate photos along with your name, address, and telephone number to:

Readers' Forum
Ideals Publications Inc.
P.O. Box 305300
Nashville, Tennessee 37230

ideals®

Publisher, Patricia A. Pingry

Editor, Michelle Prater Burke

Designer, Eve DeGrie

Pre-Press, Peggy Murphy-Jones

Copy Editor, Christine M. Landry

Editorial Assistant, Elizabeth Kea

Contributing Editors, Lansing Christman, Deana Deck, Pamela Kennedy, Nancy Skarmeas

ACKNOWLEDGMENTS

HERFORD, OLIVER. "The Dog (As Seen by the Cat)" from *The Kitten's Garden of Verses* by Oliver Herford, copyright © 1939. Reprinted by permission of Scribner, an imprint of Simon & Schuster, Inc. STRONG, PATIENCE. "Friendship" from *A Christmas Garland* by Patience Strong. Reprinted by permission of Rupert Crew Limited. Our sincere thanks to the following author whom we were unable to locate: Daniel Whitehead Hicky for "The Children in Autumn" from *Never the Nightingale.*

Friendship

Patience Strong

Time sifts our friendships and our friends,
        For time alone can be the test.
And with the passing of the years,
        We lose the false and keep the best.
And when, beyond the distant hills,
        The golden sun of life descends—
We find God's greatest gift has been
        The love of true and faithful friends.

GIVE FRIENDSHIP IDEALS TO YOUR FRIENDS

Tell your friends how much they mean to you with a gift of *Friendship Ideals.*

Order now and receive five copies of *Friendship Ideals* for just $20.95 plus $4.50 shipping and handling. That's a substantial savings over the newsstand price. Each copy comes with a large greeting envelope to make your gift extra special.

Order number 0-8249-5245-6

Send a check or money order payable to
Ideals Publications Inc. to:
Ideals Friendship
P.O. Box 305300
Nashville, Tennessee 37230-5300

For credit card orders, call toll-free:
1-800-558-4343

All orders for this item must be prepaid.